# Verses From South London

Edited by Michelle Afford

YoungWriters
First published in Great Britain in 2007 by:
Young Writers
Remus House
Coltsfoot Drive
Peterborough
PE2 9JX
Telephone: 01733 890066
Website: www.youngwriters.co.uk



SB ISBN 1 84602 732 2

# Foreword

Young Writers was established in 1991 and has been passionately devoted to the promotion of reading and writing in children and young adults ever since. The quest continues today. Young Writers remains as committed to the nurturing of poetic and literary talent as ever.

This year's Young Writers competition has proven as vibrant and dynamic as ever and we are delighted to present a showcase of the best poetry from across the UK and in some cases overseas. Each poem has been selected from a wealth of *A Pocketful Of Rhyme* entries before ultimately being published in this, our fourteenth primary school poetry series.

Once again, we have been supremely impressed by the overall quality of the entries we have received. The imagination, energy and creativity which has gone into each young writer's entry made choosing the poems a challenging and often difficult but ultimately hugely rewarding task - the general high standard of the work submitted ensured this opportunity to bring their poetry to a larger appreciative audience.

We sincerely hope you are pleased with this final collection and that you will enjoy *A Pocketful Of Rhyme Verses From South London* for many years to come.

# Contents

**Cameron House School**

Gaby Haam (10) 1
Cara Lahnstein (10) 2
Virginia Porter (11) 3
Isabella Colocci (10) 4
Phoebe Solon (10) 5
Jessie Wyman (10) 6
Hamish Frew (10) 7
Agnes Pierce Jones (9) 8
James Flory (8) 9
Margareta Zimina (9) 10
Matilda Cottrell (8) 11
Isabella Knopfler (8) 12
Matilda Wyman (8) 13
Jonathan Williams (8) 14
Tim Lahnstein (8) 15
Serena Phillips (8) 16
Toby Attard-Manche (8) 17
Olivia Dobson (8) 18
Marina Luccioni (8) 19
Henrietta Stanley (9) 20
Valentina Stefanile (9) 21
Yasmine Childs (10) 22
Charlotte Grussing (9) 23
Zahya Al-Dhabari (9) 24
Charlotte Watts (10) 25
Ambre Megnin-Aubry 26
Anna Haripersaud (9) 27

**Julian's Primary School**

Ikhlas Morrison (8) 28
Monty Coyle (8) 29
Stanley Harvey (8) 30
Beatrice Gane (8) 31
Mike Shoesmith (8) 32
Ximena Barker (9) 33
Max Goodwin (8) 34
Sarah Parkes (8) 35
Arin DeRizzio-Rahman (8) 36

Daniel Mutten (8) 37
Mahri Love (8) 38
Eve Tredwen (9) 39
James Watkins (8) 40
Laura Viana-Gardner (9) 41
Felix Lewis (8) 42
Tayo Ward-Brew (8) 43
Tyler Annon-Murray (10) 44
Monique Lewin-Blake (10) 45
Roshaan Nazir (11) 46
Martha Alexander (10) 47
Connor McCabe (10) 48
Jessica Ramos (10) 49
Anthony Clarke (10) 50
Eva McKenzie (10) 51
Jodie Hunt (10) 52
Rishaun Singh (10) 53
Michaela Bent (11) 54
Helen Da Silva (10) 55
Gabrielle Lindie (10) 56
Ellie Gray (10) 57
Aaron Hanlan (10) 58
Sarah Bowen (10) 59
Aedan Radvanyi (10) 60
Asiyah Morrison (10) 61
Jazmin Qunta (10) 62
Finn Noyes (10) 63
Dwiesha Brown (11) 64
Zaeem Hoque (7) 65
Frank White (7) 66
Maisha Zaman (9) 67
Solomon Adu (9) 68
Chanaiya Brown (9) 69
Tyra Ramnarace (9) 70
Chelsea Harvey (9) 71
Jay Dhillon (9) 72
Miles Adelaja (9) 73
Zareen Alam (9) 74
Nikki Brown (9) 75
Brandon Hanlan (9) 76
Jason Ashford (9) 77
James Wilson-Dedrick (9) 78

Lorian Beaton (9) 79
Sunil Taper (9) 80
Evandro Silva (9) 81
Tania Neacsu (9) 82
Naomi Cotton (9) 83

**Kelvin Grove Primary School**
Claudia Camacho (11) 84
Reuben Kallo (10) 85
Tia Goldring (10) 86
Panashe Enock (11) 87
Amelia Adebomi (11) 88
Patricija Rascuikeviciute (10) 89
Savannah Chan-Ellis (10) 90
Jessica Oulai (10) 91
Abdullah Cepalovic (10) 92
Aderayo Aderiye (11) 93
Amelia Bristow (11) 94
Nicole Bowman (10) 95
Marlon Ducent-Brown (11) 96
Rochelle Albert (11) 97
Kieran Pantry-Melsom (10) 98
Sarah Jinodu (11) 99
Leanne Cowan (10) 100

**Royston Primary School**
Tawanda Kazembe (7) 101
Siam Adib (8) 102
Jake Wheeler (7) 103
Chloe Wheeler (7) 104
Tamara Bailey (8) 105
Billy Best (7) 106
Charlie Cox (7) 107
Danilo Mrvaljevic (7) 108

**St Andrew's Catholic Primary School, Streatham**
Oliver Redmond (9) 109
James Moran (9) 110
Sean McGreevy (9) 111
Alex Olivia Redman (9) 112
Daniel Alphonso (10) 113

Ellie Craven (10) 114
Francesca Pereira (9) 115
George Fitzgerald (9) 116
Jake Hernandez (10) 117
Joseph Alford (10) 118
Prudence Gabriel (9) 119
Roisin Doherty (9) 120
Sandra Ofili (9) 121
Uchenna Onyeji (10) 122
Charlotte Hernandez (9) 123
Adesua Okoeguale (9) 124
Isabella Soares (9) 125
Olivia Murphy (9) 126
Dina Feseha (9) 127
Emilia Capitelli (10) 128
Megan Di Luzio (10) 129
Dejuan Markland (9) 130
Sammy Mehari (9) 131
Theresa Pillay (9) 132
Alice Beadle (10) 133
Sharlene Smith (9) 134
Javiera Martinez (10) 135
Amara Akande (9) 136
Edward Obeng-Botah (10) 137
Yasmin Campbell 138
Amir Hyder (9) 139
Sinead Moran (9) 140
Hannah Longley (9) 141
Danika Brereton (9) 142

**St Joseph's Catholic Primary School, Rotherhithe**
Stephanie Etemewei (10) 143
Ekinadose Igbinoba (10) 144
Jade Killick (10) 145
Andres Torres (11) 146
Michael Akinfisoye (10) 147
Reece Bayne (10) 148
Joseph Olaiya (10) 149
Charlie Kiely (10) 150
Joel Christofi (10) 151
Yolanda Kisenyi (11) 152

Bimpe Adeyemo (10) 153
Adebowale Adenugba (10) 154
Eleni Christofi (7) 155
Jack Roff (7) 156
Eren Ezel (8) 157
Fisayo Adenugba (8) 158
Conor Walsh (8) 159
Tasha Lohan (8) 160
Sophie Metcalf (8) 161
Mark Eastwood-Webb (8) 162

**St Margaret's Lee CE School, Lewisham**
Tessa Wade (10) 163
Annalise Morley (11) 164
Chante Roach (10) 165

**Stockwell Primary School**
Melanie Da Silva Pinto (6) 166
Nekeshia McKenzie (8) 167
Khaleda Islam (8) 168
Shaquille Davis (9) 169
Natasha Ratnayake (10) 170
Danny Smith (10) 171
Nickandra Smith (10) 172
Jordan Abbah (9) 173
Jamal Bartley (9) 174
Ellis Thomas (10) 175
Tesfa Atere (9) 176
Shannon Jackson (10) 177
Jaydene Reece-Gardner (8) 178
Alice Postans (10) 179
Kelly Tran (9) 180
Tonicha Hilder (9) 181
Neev Trehan (8) 182
Hassan Mugga (10) 183
Kevaun McKenzie (10) 184
Diana Sam (9) 185
Sashalee Biggs (8) 186
Arifur Rahman (8) 187

# The Poems

## The Magic Box

*(Based on 'Magic Box' by Kit Wright)*

I will put in the box . . .
The bubbling of a waterfall
The purring of a lonely kitten
The swish of a red fox's tail.

I will put in the box . . .
The tinkle of bells on a winter's night
The song of a sorrowful swallow,
The dust of the tiniest fairy.

I will put in the box . . .
The largest ice cream cake with a cherry on top
The twinkle of a million stars
The red of the longest sunset.

I will put in the box . . .
The blue of the water from a crystal lake
The reflection of a lily in a never-ending stream
A cloud as a pillow lined with silver.

I will put in my box . . .
The strength of a giant
The wash of a wave
The first laugh of a baby.

My box is fashioned from ice, sapphires and diamonds
With dreams on the lid and wishes in the corners
Its hinges are ruby rings.

I shall swim in my box
In the longest jacuzzi made of crystals
Then lie on a beach, the sand sparkling like stars.

**Gaby Haam (10)**
**Cameron House School**

## The Magic Box

*(Based on 'Magic Box' by Kit Wright)*

I will put in the box . . .
The friend from a long-lasting friendship
The glimpse of luminous light awakening the world
The tint of a happy child just awoken.

I will put in the box . . .
A reflection from the deep Pacific Ocean
The love of families gathering around
A soft breeze that the whole world can touch.

I will put in the box . . .
A trusting future with caring creatures
An impossible binding creation
An unforgettable life that will never end.

My box is fashioned from joy, love and sadness
With carefulness on the lid and fear in the corners
Its hinges are never alive but live forever

I will travel with my box
To the far end of the world
To the places which are filled with love
And the places which will always be there.

**Cara Lahnstein (10)**
**Cameron House School**

## The Magic Box

*(Based on 'Magic Box' by Kit Wright)*

I will put in the box . . .
The finest feather from a fire phoenix
The gentle summer breeze
The orangy-brown leaves falling to the ground.

I will put in the box . . .
The smile of my friends in the morning
The sparkling water of the Amazon River in the sun
The pink ribbon from Degas' ballet dancer.

I will put into the box . . .
The fuchsia of a fuchsia flower
The melody of a hummingbird
The colours and shapes of fireworks.

My box is fashioned from gold, silver and sapphires
With everyone's happiness on the lid and hope in the corners
Its hinges are the beak of a toucan.

I shall sing in my box
Of the joys of spring, summer, autumn and winter
Then watch and listen to the peace and serenity
The colour of the rising sun.

**Virginia Porter (11)**
**Cameron House School**

## The Magic Box

*(Based on 'Magic Box' by Kit Wright)*

I will put in the box . . .
The call of a cowboy collecting cattle
Snow circling around trees
Light reflecting on azure seas.

I will put in the box . . .
A light breeze on a meadow
A baby's first steps
Wild horses galloping along.

I will put in the box . . .
Snow in the summer
A moon made of biscuit
A parallel universe.

My box is fashioned from fire, wind and water
With clouds on the lid and joy in the corners
Its hinges are snakes coiled up into springs.

I shall sail on my box
Through turquoise waters and giant waves
I'll land on the top of the tallest mountain
Wind gently brushing my hair.

**Isabella Colocci (10)**
**Cameron House School**

## In My Box

*(Based on 'Magic Box' by Kit Wright)*

I will put in my box . . .
The coldness of a winter's night
Laughter of a child with its mother
A rushing of a waterfall.

A will put in my box . . .
A single shining tear from a baby
Dew from a blade of grass in the early morning
A leap from a newborn frog.

My box is fashioned from ivy from the palace walls
Gold leaves from 'The Happy Prince'
With the world's peace on the lid.

I shall travel in my box
To unknown countries
Then tell the world
Of my wondrous adventures.

**Phoebe Solon (10)**
**Cameron House School**

# The Magic Box

*(Based on 'Magic Box' by Kit Wright)*

I will put in my box . . .
The hollow sound of a willow tree swaying on a winter's day
A witch's sneer on Hallowe'en
A sharp, dangerous dagger from a dragon's mouth.

I will put in my box . . .
An ebony star from a jet-black night
The darkest light from the gloomiest sun
The meanest frown from Father Christmas.

I will put in my box . . .
The sharpest point from the evil Devil
And the scariest mask from the Dead Sea
The loudest scream from a baby.

My box is fashioned from skeletons, vampires and ghosts
Its hinges are dirty, sharp, long, pointed claws of werewolves
With nightmares on the lid and in the corner is a little hope.

**Jessie Wyman (10)**
**Cameron House School**

## Parallel World

Football flashing, boots are bashing,
One-nil down, we don't have to frown,
Two-nil down, it's laughing town,
No one cares if we lose this match
Or each boy if, from the team
He is scratched,
Everything's the opposite here and now
Let's take a bow, we're happy now.

**Hamish Frew (10)**
**Cameron House School**

## My Senses

*Love*
Love is pink like a piglet
It sounds like kissing
It tastes like home-made brownies
It looks like a new member of the family
It feels like cashmere gloves
Love reminds me of my family.

**Agnes Pierce Jones (9)**
**Cameron House School**

## My Senses

*Laughter*
Laughter is red like a tomato
It sounds like a big giggle
It smells like lots of chocolate
It tastes like a plateful of sauce
It looks like a big celebration
It feels like lots of air
Laughter reminds me of the funniest thing ever.

**James Flory (8)**
**Cameron House School**

## My Senses

*Love* is pink like a rose
It sounds like the miaow of a kitten
It smells like a beautiful flower
It looks like a heart
It feels like a kitten
Love reminds me of my boyfriend.

*Happiness* is blue like the sky
It sounds like a little twinkle
It smells like a little spaghetti piece
It looks like a pool of water
It feels really cold
Happiness reminds me of a happy life.

*Fun* is light green like a turtle
It sounds like a little light wind
It smells like the sea
It looks like a crown
It feels like a fluffy coat
Fun reminds me of silly jokes.

**Margareta Zimina (9)**
**Cameron House School**

## Love

Love is turquoise like a diamond
It sounds like the purr of a kitten
It smells like a bakery shop
It tastes like a chocolate cake
It looks like a fresh pack of roses
It feels like a cotton pom-pom
Love reminds me of every thrill
That your life has hit you with.

**Matilda Cottrell (8)**
**Cameron House School**

## My Senses

*Fun* is blue like clear blue sky
It sounds like the tap of a playful puppy
It tastes like ice cream, cold and sweet
It looks like a puppy running on luscious grass
It feels like soft, dry fur
Fun reminds me of jumping into the pool!

*Love* is pink like strawberry love hearts
It sounds like church bells ringing
It smells like lavender
It tastes like fresh berries
It looks like a peaceful, trickling stream
It feels like floating cloud fluff
It reminds me of my mummy and daddy putting me to bed.

*Darkness* is mauve like the sunset
It sounds like dancing and silence
It smells like burnt toast
It tastes like dry coldness
It looks like a dark, deserted place
It feels like something unknown
Darkness reminds me of waking up in the morning to a new day!

**Isabella Knopfler (8)**
**Cameron House School**

## My Senses

Love is pink like a heart
It sounds like a bee collecting pollen
It smells like flowers
It tastes like honey
It looks like a field full of flowers
It feels like a pillow as soft as cashmere
Love reminds me of my family.

Fun is orange like a friend
It smells like the park
It tastes like sweets
It looks like the beach on a sunny day
It feels like a dolly
Fun reminds me of a funfair.

Sadness is blue like the sea
It sounds like rain
It smells like strawberries
It tastes like tears
It looks like a puppy crying
Sadness reminds me of my family dying.

**Matilda Wyman (8)**
**Cameron House School**

## Fun

Fun is blue like the sky
It sounds like when you are playing in the sea
It smells like a meadow
It tastes like ice cream
It looks like a circus
It feels like being in the sun
It reminds me of being in the Mediterranean Sea
And being in Switzerland for the summer.

**Jonathan Williams (8)**
**Cameron House School**

## My Senses

Fun is yellow like the sun
It sounds like kids laughing
It smells like slimy jelly
It tastes like hot bacon
It looks like people running around
It feels like melting ice cream
Fun reminds me of happy children.

Love is red like a heart
It sounds like people cheering
It smells like roses
It tastes like orange juice
It looks like a teddy bear
It feels like a warm blanket
Love reminds me of my mum.

Laughter is pink chewing gum
It sounds like a happy song
It smells like an apple
It tastes like chocolate
It feels like a bouncy castle
Laughter reminds me of my grandma.

**Tim Lahnstein (8)**
**Cameron House School**

## My Senses

Love is the colour of pink love hearts
It sounds like a little songbird singing at dusk
It smells like a bar of melted chocolate
It tastes like the first ripe strawberry of the summer
It looks like the face of an angel
It feels like being wrapped in a cashmere blanket
Love reminds me of when my sister was born.

Happiness is the colour of the tranquil blue sea
It sounds like rushing water
It smells like a field full of lavender
It tastes like mint ice cream melting in my mouth
It looks like my sister paddling in the sea
It feels like diving into a swimming pool on a hot summer's day
Happiness reminds me of swimming with dolphins.

Fun is a wild purple
It sounds like my sister chuckling
It smells like candyfloss
It tastes like a fizzy drink
It looks like my sister throwing her food on the clean floor
It feels like my dad throwing me up in the air
Fun reminds me of my family.

**Serena Phillips (8)**
**Cameron House School**

## Love

Love is all colours of the rainbow
It smells like roses
It sounds like a hummingbird
It feels like a silk blanket
It reminds me of having family fun
It tastes like apple pie.

**Toby Attard-Manche (8)**
**Cameron House School**

## My Senses

Hate is the colour of black
It sounds like the roar of a dragon
It smells like the ashes of a fire
It tastes like burnt bits of toast
It looks like a world of black spiders
It feels like a bed of spikes
Hate reminds me of volcanoes.

Fun is purple like a flower
It sounds like children laughing
It smells like chocolate
It tastes like marshmallows
It looks like a puppy
It feels like smooth rock
It reminds me of happiness.

Laughter is the colour of light blue, like the sky
It sounds like birds singing
It smells like flowers
It tastes like lollipops
It looks like the sun
It feels like a smooth pillow
It reminds me of fun.

**Olivia Dobson (8)**
**Cameron House School**

## My Senses

Love is red like a heart
It sounds like a clarinet
It smells like a rose
It tastes like a sweet sugar candy
It looks like a puppy chasing a butterfly in a big field of flowers
It feels like never-ending happiness
Love reminds me of my loyal black dog.

Happiness is yellow like the ever-brightening sun
It sounds like a harp going on and on
It smells like chlorine on a wet towel, a reminder of a fun-filled pool play day
It tastes like brownie-flavoured fudge
It looks like three friends laughing while playing their own made-up game
It feels like a vibrating balloon getting bigger and bigger, but never bursting in your chest
Happiness reminds me of my best friends, Emma and Anna Grey.

Laughter is orange like a smiling Jack-o'-lantern
It sounds like the jingling of bells
It tastes like freshly squeezed oranges
It smells like lemon tart
It looks like kids having a water balloon fight
It feels like a strong, never-ending set of vibrations
Laughter reminds me of animals, wild and tame, running free.

**Marina Luccioni (8)**
**Cameron House School**

## Dave Dirt's Smelly Socks

His socks smelt like a gigantic pike
A rotten egg, a pongy peg,
A lump of mould, a boy with a cold
A woman's filthy hair, a man's underwear
A lump of soil, a teenager's boil
Three-day-old porridge, my gran, Morridge
Well, that's Dave Dirt for you.

**Henrietta Stanley (9)**
**Cameron House School**

## Dave's Birthday

On Dave's birthday
What a mess!
Cakes and socks and cuddly toys
And little sister, Bess.

On Dave's birthday
Kirke came over
And Dave Dirt gave him a makeover
In this way Kirke refused a sleepover!

On Dave's birthday
It was food-fight time
Covering Bess in jelly and lime!

Mashed potato on the wall
Happy birthday to you all!

**Valentina Stefanile (9)**
**Cameron House School**

## Naughty Dave Dirt

Dave had a sleepover with all his friends
They made a huge mess
Dave thought it was the best
They made slug pie
They also stayed up all night
This was great because Mother was nowhere in sight
'Go back to sleep, now,' his mother had said,
But did she really think they were going to stay in bed?
'If you make a mess, you'll tidy it up in the morning.'
Does she really have to be so boring?

**Yasmine Childs (10)**
**Cameron House School**

## Dave Dirt Is Hungry

Dave Dirt would die
For a piece of chicken-fried pie.

He would break his arm
For eggs from a barn.

He would make a pledge
For a chocolate wedge.

He would forever say, 'Pretty please,'
For a lump of cottage cheese.

He would break his mum's crystal clear chandelier
For a drink of root beer.

He would give up graffiti
For a sweetie.

He would get a college degree
For a sweet pea.

He would shave his head
For a slice of bread.

He would lie on a railroad track
For a small snack.

He would become a glamorous girl scout
For a tasty trout.

Chicken, duck, turkey too
He'd even make a sister stew!

**Charlotte Grussing (9)**
**Cameron House School**

## Fairy Dust

If you see a shooting star
The fairy queen will not be far.

In the middle of the night
The moon, for your path, will shine her light.

And if you have a glass of morning dew
All your wishes may come true.

So always feel as high as a kite
And you'll shine with all your might.

**Zahya Al-Dhabari (9)**
**Cameron House School**

## My Lizard

My lizard is very sweet
Unlike the parakeet.

He runs up the wall
For that lizard, there's no time to stall.

He's scaly and bumpy
Luckily, not grumpy.

And when you hold him in your hands
He runs away like quicksand . . .

**Charlotte Watts (10)**
**Cameron House School**

## Dave Dirt At School

When Dave Dirt was at school
He was quite a fool
That little lad
Was very, very bad
He would never do his work
The teacher said, 'What a jerk!'
He was very thin
Therefore he ate what was in the school bin
He even put a snake
On Ben's birthday cake!

**Ambre Megnin-Aubry**
**Cameron House School**

## Dave Dirt's Socks

Dave had a pair of socks
He covered them with candyfloss
Then put them in a silvery box
All lined in silky moss.

After a while he opened his box
To find that pair of socks
Smelling like stale cauliflower
Then said to himself, 'Oh bother!'

**Anna Haripersaud (9)**
**Cameron House School**

## The Writer Of This Poem

*(Based on 'The Writer of this Poem' by Roger McGough)*

The writer of this poem is as strong as the Minotaur
As calming as a queen
As intelligent as a computer
As crazy as a frog.

As outgoing as can be
As smooth as a frog's scale (which is impossible to see)
As sharp as a spike
As cheeky as a monkey.

As soft as a pillow
As tall as a brachiosaurus
As fast as the speed of light (which is a true sight)
As mad as a wild man.

The writer of this poem is as stern as can be
He's one out of six billion
So the poem says.

**Ikhlas Morrison (8)**
**Julian's Primary School**

## The Writer Of This Poem

*(Based on 'The Writer of this Poem' by Roger McGough)*

The writer of this poem is as tall as a tree
As cheeky as a monkey, as strong as a whale
As mad as a fish, as smelly as a fart
As intelligent as a computer, as bold as a stone wall
*'The writer of this poem*
*Never ceases to amaze*
*He's one in a million billion*
*(Or so the poem says!)'.*

**Monty Coyle (8)**
**Julian's Primary School**

## The Writer Of This Poem

*(Based on 'The Writer of this Poem' by Roger McGough)*

The writer of this poem is . . .
Stronger than an elephant
Faster than an eagle
Taller than a tree

Softer than a teddy bear
Smarter than a brain
Dumber than a mule
Louder than a drain

As flat as concrete
Cleaner than water
As bold as a knight
More demanding than a king

*'The writer of this poem*
*Never ceases to amaze*
*He's one in a million billion*
*(Or so the poem says)'.*

**Stanley Harvey (8)**
**Julian's Primary School**

# The Writer Of This Poem

*(Based on 'The Writer of this Poem' by Roger McGough)*

The writer of this poem is . . .
As strong as an elephant
As quick as a flash
As soft as a feather

As cheeky as a monkey
as posh as a restaurant
As cuddly as a cushion
As handsome as a lady

The writer of this poem is
As smart as can be
As hot as the sun
As tall as a skyscraper

*'The writer of this poem*
*Never ceases to amaze*
*She's one in a million billion*
*(Or so the poem says)'.*

**Beatrice Gane (8)**
**Julian's Primary School**

## The Writer Of This Poem

*(Based on 'The Writer of this Poem' by Roger McGough)*

The writer of this poem is . . .
Taller than a giant
As swift as a cheetah
As clever as a scientist

As sharp as a race dog
As amazing as a magician
As cheeky as a monkey
As sly as a fox

As active as a dog
As funny as a clown
As sporty as an athlete
As strong as a brick

*'The writer of this poem*
*Never ceases to amaze*
*He's one in a million billion*
*(Or so the poem says)'.*

**Mike Shoesmith (8)**
**Julian's Primary School**

## The Writer Of This Poem

*(Based on 'The Writer of this Poem' by Roger McGough)*

The writer of this poem is
Pinker than a pig
As arty as an artichoke
As tasty as a fig

As pretty as a princess
As naughty as a nut
As handy as a hula Hoop
As crazy as a cut

As tricky as a math's sum
As jumpy as a joo
As soggy as a sausage
As lazy as a loo

She's dumber than a doughnut
As clever as a carrot
As angry as an apricot
As potty as a parrot

*'The writer of this poem*
*Never ceases to amaze*
*She's one in a million billion*
*(Or so the poem says)'.*

**Ximena Barker (9)**
**Julian's Primary School**

## The Writer Of This Poem

*(Based on 'The Writer of this Poem' by Roger McGough)*

The writer of this poem is . . .
As strong as a tree
As loud as a gorilla
As fast as a bee

As bold as a boxing glove
As sharp as a cheetah
As keen as the north wind
Bigger than a heater

*'The writer of this poem*
*Never ceases to amaze*
*He's one in a million billion*
*(Or so the poem says)'.*

**Max Goodwin (8)**
**Julian's Primary School**

## The Writer Of This Poem

*(Based on 'The Writer of this Poem' by Roger McGough)*

The writer of this poem is . . .
As cheeky as can be
Has an extraordinary imagination
As you can see

As difficult as a grumpy dog
As smart as a snake
As dramatic as a dragon
As delicious as a cake

As naughty as a nuisance
As tall as a dragon's den
As bright as a bunch of flowers
As loud as a group of men

*'The writer of this poem*
*Never ceases to amaze*
*She's one in a million billion*
*(Or so the poem says)'.*

**Sarah Parkes (8)**
**Julian's Primary School**

## The Writer Of This Poem

*(Based on 'The Writer of this Poem' by Roger McGough)*

The writer of this poem is . . .
As tall as a tree
As strong as a brick
As stingy as a bee

As cheeky as a monkey
As beautiful as a rose
As fast as a cheetah
As wet as a hose

As bold as a boxing glove
As sharp as a nib
As strong as scaffolding
As tricky as a fib

The writer of this poem
Isn't really any of that stuff
But actually, from my point
I think it is good enough.

**Arin DeRizzio-Rahman (8)**
**Julian's Primary School**

## The Writer Of This Poem

*(Based on 'The Writer of this Poem' by Roger McGough)*

The writer of this poem is . . .
As sharp as glass
I'm as bright as the sun
I'm as intelligent as can be
I'm as tall as a tree
I'm as big as a millionaire

I'm as bold as a bowling ball
I'm as sly as a fox
I'm as clean as a chemist shop
I'm as spotty as a parrot

*'The writer of this poem*
*Never ceases to amaze*
*He's one in a million billion*
*(Or so the poem says)'.*

**Daniel Mutten (8)**
**Julian's Primary School**

## The Writer Of This Poem

*(Based on 'The Writer of this Poem' by Roger McGough)*

The writer of this poem is . . .
Stronger than the sea
As beautiful as a rose
(Without the thorns)
As clever as can be

As fast as a cheetah
As tall as a tree
As slim as a twig
As neat as can be

As swift as an eagle
As mighty as a horse
As dramatic as an actor
She doesn't use a lot of force

She's really, really gorgeous
She can walk to the end of the rainbow
She's really, really cute
As cheeky as a monkey, you know.

The writer of this poem
Only sometimes causes trouble
Let's hope there's no more drama
And hope she doesn't have a double.

**Mahri Love (8)**
**Julian's Primary School**

## The Writer Of This Poem

*(Based on 'The Writer of this Poem' by Roger McGough)*

The writer of this poem is . . .
As beautiful as a rose
As sporty as a cheetah
And is great with clothes

As intelligent as a cat
As cute as a baby
As tall as a top hat
As fit as a carrot

As strong as scaffolding
As smart as a brain
As fast as a cheetah
As flexible as rubber

*'The writer of this poem*
*Never ceases to amaze*
*She's one in a million billion*
*(Or so the poem says)'.*

**Eve Tredwen (9)**
**Julian's Primary School**

## The Writer Of This Poem

*(Based on 'The Writer of this Poem' by Roger McGough)*

The writer of this poem is . . .
As swift as a cheetah
As tall as a mountain
As sharp as a race dog

As cheeky as a monkey
As clever as a chimpanzee
As amazing as a magician
As sly as a fox

As strong as a rhino
As funny as a clown
As evil as a devil
As high as the sky

The writer of this poem
Isn't really any of that stuff
But actually, from my point
I think it's good enough.

**James Watkins (8)**
**Julian's Primary School**

## The Writer Of This Poem

*(Based on 'The Writer of this Poem' by Roger McGough)*

The writer of this poem is . . .
As soft as a pillow
As cheeky as a monkey
As flexible as a willow

As big as an elephant
As swift as a cheetah
As strong as a brick
I'm a very hard beater

As soft as a cloud
As tall as a tree
As bold as a bubble
As big as a bee

*'The writer of this poem*
*Never ceases to amaze*
*He's one in a million billion*
*(Or so the poem says)'.*

**Laura Viana-Gardner (9)**
**Julian's Primary School**

## The Writer Of This Poem

*(Based on 'The Writer of this Poem' by Roger McGough)*

The writer of this poem is . . .
As quick as a flash
I am as cheeky as a monkey
I am as strong as an elephant
I am as sporty as can be

I am as big as a tree
I am as long as a train
I am as mighty as a god
I am as smart as a brain

I am as bouncy as a kangaroo
I am as bold as a bubble
I am as soft as a kitten
I am as tough as a muscle

I am as hot as the sun
I am as tricky as a shark
I am as sharp as a needle
I am as loud as a bark.

**Felix Lewis (8)**
**Julian's Primary School**

## The Writer Of This Poem

*(Based on 'The Writer of this Poem' by Roger McGough)*

The writer of this poem is . . .
As cheeky as a monkey
As bouncy as a kangaroo
As fast as a cheetah
And the crocodiles go, 'Boo-hoo-hoo!'

As tall as the sky
As tough as a rhino
As daft as a donkey
As bright as the sun

The writer of this poem
Is never ever seen
Even though he looks grand
(Although, I think so).

**Tayo Ward-Brew (8)**
**Julian's Primary School**

## A Frisbee

A frisbee
It's a toy that's almost 2D
Fun, gliding, playful
Like a flying saucer gliding through the air
Like a roundabout in the playground
It makes me feel cheerful
As cheerful as someone who's won the lottery
The way it glides makes me want to fly.

**Tyler Annon-Murray (10)**
**Julian's Primary School**

## The Ocean

Covering the Earth and keeping it warm
Rough, enormous and loud
As rough as a hurricane
Sometimes as smooth as velvet
Cold as ice
A big blanket
The ocean
I like to swim in it on a hot summer's day.

**Monique Lewin-Blake (10)**
**Julian's Primary School**

## The Stars

The stars
Brightening the night
Beautiful, bright, gorgeous
As bright as a pair of headlights on a car at night
Like miniature moons
I feel myself become dim in front of them
As dim as a circuit with half a battery
They make me think of God
Who created all these beautiful stars.
The stars.

**Roshaan Nazir (11)**
**Julian's Primary School**

## What Is A Friend?

A friend is an angel sent down from Heaven
A friend's smile is a sunbeam shining on you
A friend is a clown standing on its head making you laugh
A friend is a soft armchair in a quiet room.

**Martha Alexander (10)**
**Julian's Primary School**

## Flamingos

Flamingos
The greater flamingos are the tallest
Tall, pink, pretty
Pink as a milkshake
Their necks as bendy as a piece of Blu-tack
I feel sleepy because they look like pillows
A soft place to rest my head
Flamingos
They are happy birds.

**Connor McCabe (10)**
**Julian's Primary School**

## Portugal

Portugal
A small country
Colourful, adventurous, clean
As green as a huge splodgy cake
As hot as a burning potato
As clean as the clear blue sky
Portugal, my heart's desire
Portugal, everything's on fire
1, 2, 3, 4 . . . *Portugal!*

**Jessica Ramos (10)**
**Julian's Primary School**

## My Mum

My mum
She looks after me
Kind, peaceful, funny
She's as pretty as a picture
She makes me happy
I love my mum.

**Anthony Clarke (10)**
**Julian's Primary School**

## The Stars

The stars
Fiery balls of gas
Shining, twinkling, amazing
Like the eyes of angels watching us sleep
I feel I am safe with them watching
And the biggest keeps watch during the day
The stars
They've seen the whole of time.

**Eva McKenzie (10)**
**Julian's Primary School**

## Butterflies

Butterflies
Flutter around
Colourful, pretty, small
Like beautiful diamonds
As colourful as a rainbow
Seeing them makes me smile
Butterflies
I like to watch them float around in the midday air.

**Jodie Hunt (10)**
**Julian's Primary School**

## An Elephant

An elephant
An elephant never forgets
Big, ferocious, massive
Strong like a steel wall
Like a powerful robot
It makes me feel as small as an ant
An elephant
Makes me think how small humans are.

**Rishaun Singh (10)**
**Julian's Primary School**

## What Is . . . The Rain?

The rain is a teardrop falling from the sky
It is a cloudy face going to cry
It is a dropping bluebird trying to fly
It is baby-blue paint falling from high.

**Michaela Bent (11)**
**Julian's Primary School**

## Portugal

Portugal
A big peaceful country
Nice, sunny, quiet
Like a calm ocean on a still day
It makes me feel proud and excited
Portugal
Portugal
Portugal is where people like to live.

**Helen Da Silva (10)**
**Julian's Primary School**

## Hamsters

They're rats, but smaller
Sweet, cute and fluffy
Like stones carved from angels
Like pebbles painted in colours
I feel happy and supported
As happy as the moon in the night sky
Hamsters
Hamsters keep me happy.

**Gabrielle Lindie (10)**
**Julian's Primary School**

## The Weather

Raindrops are shiny tears from a giant
Snowflakes are icing sugar on a sponge cake
Sun is a drink of orange juice on a blue tablecloth
Thunder is a rumbling tummy before lunch
Mist is an old woman going blind.

**Ellie Gray (10)**
**Julian's Primary School**

## The Lion

The lion
Runs faster than 100mph
Proud, fast, powerful
Like a tornado
Like a king of the jungle
Fabulous but scary
Makes me feel like a tiny ant in front of a human
The lion
What a fantastic creature.

**Aaron Hanlan (10)**
**Julian's Primary School**

## An Angel

An angel
As pretty as a goddess
Gorgeous, charming, delicate
Like a butterfly flying through the sky
As light as a feather
Thinking of one makes me feel peaceful
As calm as the pale blue sky
An angel.

**Sarah Bowen (10)**
**Julian's Primary School**

## The Emirates Stadium

The Emirates Stadium
A glorious artefact
Incredible, magnificent, extraordinary
As strong as the Wall of China
Like a football pitch in Heaven
It makes me feel blessed
It makes me feel like king of the football world
The Emirates Stadium
Makes me think of Heaven.

**Aedan Radvanyi (10)**
**Julian's Primary School**

## The Monkey

The monkey
Lives in the jungle
Swift, agile, cheeky
Like a fast-moving stick
As fast as a cheetah
They make me feel clumsy
Like a big foot in an ant town
The monkey
Reminds me of a ninja.

**Asiyah Morrison (10)**
**Julian's Primary School**

## Ireland

Ireland
Dublin is the capital city
Peaceful, friendly, beautiful
Like a green sheet covering the floor
As calm as a swan
Seeing its beauty makes me feel relaxed
Like a bird in the sky
Ireland
It makes us think of how friendly we can be.

**Jazmin Qunta (10)**
**Julian's Primary School**

## Sharks

Sharks
Meat-eating fish
Scary, ferocious, fearsome
They scare the life out of me
Sharks
The most fearsome fish of the sea.

**Finn Noyes (10)**
**Julian's Primary School**

## What Is . . . The Rain?

The rain is blue drops of paint
Tears of joy from the sky
Refreshing cold water
It is ink from the sky
Like clouds are crying.

**Dwiesha Brown (11)**
**Julian's Primary School**

## My Brother

My brother is my best friend although at times we fight
He kicks and I punch and sometimes he even bites
My brother is my best friend although he steals my stuff
I yell and shout and tell him, 'Enough is enough!'
My brother is my friend, at night we share a bed
I watch him sleep silently and think of the fun ahead.

**Zaeem Hoque (7)**
**Julian's Primary School**

## Wild Cats

Wild cats are quick and fast
Wild cats have smooth, fluffy fur
There are so many types of wild cats
When men go hunting, some can't catch them but others
can catch wild cats
Wild cats have very sharp canines for ripping through flesh
Wild cats live in many countries
Wild cats mate in spring
When they have cubs the cubs are very cute
They are my favourite animals
Wild cats are absolutely amazing.

**Frank White (7)**
**Julian's Primary School**

## Limerick

There was a young girl called Mabel
Who had a very big stable
She went in the jungle
To build a bundle
And she had a very long table.

**Maisha Zaman (9)**
**Julian's Primary School**

## Untitled

There once was a kangaroo
Who found a gigantic shoe
He went to the shop
And bought a lollipop
That blew him away to Peru.

**Solomon Adu (9)**
**Julian's Primary School**

## There Once . . .

There once was a lady called Ms Brown
Who always had a massive big frown
So she tried to smile
But her big brother Kyle
Said she looked like a funny clown.

**Chanaiya Brown (9)**
**Julian's Primary School**

## Limerick

There was a young girl called Mabel
Who lived in a lovely big stable
She watched TV
And ate jelly
And that is the story of Mabel.

**Tyra Ramnarace (9)**
**Julian's Primary School**

## A Girl Called Kate

There was a young lady called Kate
Who was always very, very late
She missed the bus
And made a fuss
And no one wanted to be her mate.

**Chelsea Harvey (9)**
**Julian's Primary School**

## Mr Robert

There was an old man called Robert
Who woke up after he was clobbered
He'd hurt his head
His face was red
But he never really seemed bothered.

**Jay Dhillon (9)**
**Julian's Primary School**

## Limerick

There was a young girl called Mabel
Who loved her new toy stable
She liked to play
Every day
And that's the story of Mabel.

**Miles Adelaja (9)**
**Julian's Primary School**

## Limerick About A Horse

There was a young girl called Mabel
Who worked in a very nice stable
She cuddled horses
And took them to courses
Mabel was unable to buy them new stables.

**Zareen Alam (9)**
**Julian's Primary School**

## A Boy Called Jim

There once was a boy called Jim
He loved to look in the bins
He found a mouse
He took it to his house
And scared his friend Tim.

**Nikki Brown (9)**
**Julian's Primary School**

## The Boy Called Fred

There once was a boy called Fred
He always stayed in bed
He wouldn't get up
He slept with his duck
Until his mother turned red.

**Brandon Hanlan (9)**
**Julian's Primary School**

## Stake Boy

There was a young girl called Mabel
Who sat on the edge of a table
She forgot to take off the red label
She started to watch the TV cable
That's the poem about Mabel.

**Jason Ashford (9)**
**Julian's Primary School**

## Limerick

There once was a kangaroo
Who lived in a giant zoo
Cause number one
He sucked his thumb
And didn't know what to do.

**James Wilson-Dedrick (9)**
**Julian's Primary School**

## Limerick

There was a young girl called Rose
Who went to go and propose
He said, 'No,
Away you go,'
*I'll never propose again, I suppose.*

**Lorian Beaton (9)**
**Julian's Primary School**

## Limerick

There once was a very old man
Who had a terribly mad pan
It gurgled and burped
Oh, what a twerp
He had a wicked plan.

**Sunil Taper (9)**
**Julian's Primary School**

## Old Man Phil

There was an old man called Phil
He had to pay a big bill
He said, 'No way,'
And ran away
And kicked a great big till.

**Evandro Silva (9)**
**Julian's Primary School**

## Untitled

'Oh monkey, oh where have you been?'
'I went to see the Queen.
I sat under thrones,
And ate lots of bones
And now the Queen I have seen!'

**Tania Neacsu (9)**
**Julian's Primary School**

## Limerick

There once was a man called Phil
Who paid an enormous bill
He could not afford
Really anything more
And just had to blame his wife, Jill.

**Naomi Cotton (9)**
**Julian's Primary School**

## A Best Friend

A best friend is an angel
coming down from Heaven to a school.
She's as sweet as a puppy,
the person of your dreams.

A best friend is the sun
that brings heat to everyone.
She's as friendly as a bear,
the person you think about all the time.

A best friend is a fairy
you always go flying with.
She's as cute as a rabbit
you're glad that she's with you.

A best friend makes the clouds go away
and the sun come out.
She's as gentle as a cat,
the person that you'll always want to keep.

**Claudia Camacho (11)**
**Kelvin Grove Primary School**

## Who Is My Mum?

My mum is a diamond on Earth,
She is a soul never to be touched,
She is a plant that needs water to survive,
She is a treasure chest at the bottom of the sea full of gold.

**Reuben Kallo (10)**
**Kelvin Grove Primary School**

## The Blue Cat

I am a big puddle of blue fur,
I am as blue as the Pacific Ocean,
I am a blue cloud in the kitty sky,
I am as blue as the sky and beyond,
I am a blue river in a planet of cats,
I am as blue as a lake,
I am the blue diamond of the night,
I am the blue crystal in the ring,
I am as blue as a waterfall,
I am as blue as a stream.

I am a blue rug on the floor,
I am a blue hamburger bun, uncooked,
I am a blue angel in cat's heaven,
I am as blue as a blue bowling ball,
Basically, I am blue!

**Tia Goldring (10)**
**Kelvin Grove Primary School**

## What Is My Mum?

My mum is a big great love bug that you can't shake off.
My mum is a great huge star that shines bright in the sky.
My mum is the great sun that chases the clouds away.

**Panashe Enock (11)**
**Kelvin Grove Primary School**

## What Is A Bird?

A bird is an echo flying in the sky.
A bird is a shooting star,
gliding through the air.
A bird is the mother of nests,
that sleeps in the trees.
It is a bread-eating machine,
pecking with its sharp beak.

A bird is a little dragon,
landing in the trees.
A bird is a jet plane,
soaring higher and higher.
It is a swooping eagle,
grabbing you when you don't expect it.
It is a bird-shaped cloud,
coming to life.

A bird is a feathery balloon,
rising into the air.
A bird is a sheet of paper,
being dragged by the wind.
It is a black flying leaf,
floating in the sky.
A bird is a feather,
falling to the ground.

**Amelia Adebomi (11)**
**Kelvin Grove Primary School**

## My Fluffy Cat

Once I had a fluffy cat,
Who always laid on my mat.
He used to lay near the warm fire and sleep,
I always peeked behind the door,
When I came inside he would always leap.
All he wanted was to sleep all day,
I didn't know why.
So I decided to play but he would just lay!
What happened to him?

**Patricija Rascuikeviciute (10)**
**Kelvin Grove Primary School**

## Cheeky Monkey

Cheeky monkey loved to swing,
because it was his favourite thing.
To and fro from tree to tree,
that's where Cheeky loved to be.
At every race he'd always win,
and carry around his cheeky grin.
But one day Cheeky began to drop,
so that day Cheeky had to stop.

**Savannah Chan-Ellis (10)**
**Kelvin Grove Primary School**

## Those Babies

Those babies are speechless,
Everyone thinks they are cute,
But I'll tell you the truth,
Those babies are little devils
That cry all day.

Those babies give stress and depression,
How do you handle them?
Those babies might look like teddies
But they're the evil kind.
Those babies look like grandmas
Because they have no teeth.

Those babies are like sour cherries
Those babies act like the victim
When they are the suspect.
So now you must see,
Those babies are driving me crazy.

**Jessica Oulai (10)**
**Kelvin Grove Primary School**

## Do You Want My Dog?

This is a poem about my dog.
You might like it or you might not.
This is how my poem goes
My dog is as fierce as a lion,
He thinks there is a place called Zion!
He is skinny, hairy and has red eyes,
He likes to eat a lot of pies.

My dog will never eat his food,
Only if you give him pies.
My dog hates old people,
He gets his pies from a shop called Lidl.

My dog is a piece of paper floating along the bright blue sea.
You have to take him for a walk three times a day.
You have to let him sleep on your bed,
If you don't you'll have a sore head.

My dog is as white as a piece of paper.
He likes to watch a lot of TV,
So someone tell me,
Do you want my dog?

**Abdullah Cepalovic (10)**
**Kelvin Grove Primary School**

## Motorbike Fool

My name is Spike,
Motorcycles are what I like.
Along the road I speed,
Yep, that's my need.
I grease my hair with engine oil,
Most of my clothes are made out of foil.
Some people say I'm a geek instead of cool,
Then I shout out again, I'm a motorcycle fool!
My mum's a biker, my dad's one too,
We're on the road 24/7, I never go to the loo.
I stopped to get a bit of corn,
Then I said to myself, 'A biker isn't made,
A biker is born!'

**Aderayo Aderiye (11)**
**Kelvin Grove Primary School**

## The Wolf Of Barnley Bay

Why do they run?
I'm just having a little fun.
As I slip through the wood,
As silent as the grass itself,
As black as the night,
I hear a voice, sense a smell!
A small child is coming,
A girl's voice, as timid as a mouse!
'Could the wolf pounce in this very wood, Papa?'
'Yes, my child, of that he could.'
Now the voice was loud and clear,
I felt the urge from a hellish pit,
Reaching, reaching, pushing
And pouncing
That is why they run.

**Amelia Bristow (11)**
**Kelvin Grove Primary School**

## The Black Cat

My black cat jumps like a kangaroo,
My black cat is as fast as a cheetah,
My black cat is as clever as a computer,
My black cat is cuddly like a teddy bear,
My black cat is as furry as a bunny rabbit
And my black cat's eyes are so bright
Like the stars at night-time.

My black cat is cute like a baby,
My black cat is like a toy,
My black cat is as smart as a dictionary,
My black cat is as good as gold,
My black cat's head is as round as a ball
And my black cat is as strong as an ogre.

**Nicole Bowman (10)**
**Kelvin Grove Primary School**

## The Black Dog

I met a black dog on the street,
He was as handsome as a prince,
His eyes were as yellow as the sun.
But I saw him talking to a knight,
He was as black as the sky,
He did look cute.
Then I saw female dogs and girls,
Running after him.
He took off into the air.
He dropped down like a balloon being let down.
Then he went into a castle
And pretended to be a knight.

**Marlon Ducent-Brown (11)**
**Kelvin Grove Primary School**

## The Magical Cat

He is mighty like a knight,
His claws are as sharp as a knife.
He flies to space and has a laugh with his mates.
Argues with human beings,
Fat like a ball,
He's always fighting in the hall in school.
Watches TV, eats junk food,
Farts in class
And drinks out of a glass.
Powerful like a dragon,
Talks really loud,
He even screams like a girl
When the wolves howl, howl, howl.
Runs like a chicken,
Dances every day.
Small like a mouse,
Squeaks in his house.
His big mum said,
'Come eat some kidney and liver instead.'

**Rochelle Albert (11)**
**Kelvin Grove Primary School**

## The Two Dogs

I have a dog called Mikey,
When he's wet his fur gets spiky.
I took him to the park,
We bumped into the dog next door, called Spark.
They looked the same,
I called Mikey's name
And a boy said, 'What?'

**Kieran Pantry-Melsom (10)**
**Kelvin Grove Primary School**

## What Is My Mum?

My mum is the light and shining armour of my soul.
My mum is the fertiliser and plant food that nourishes me.
My mum is the heart in me that pumps my blood.

**Sarah Jinodu (11)**
**Kelvin Grove Primary School**

## The Munching Rabbit

We have a rabbit called Willoughby Woo,
who runs around the house; doesn't know what to do.
He chases the cat, but shouldn't do that
because when she's annoyed she scratches him back.
He jumps on the sofa, he chews the chairs,
he munches the woodwork and nibbles the stairs.
My mum, though she loves him, doesn't know what to do
about this munching rabbit, Willoughby Woo.

**Leanne Cowan (10)**
**Kelvin Grove Primary School**

## Pear Poem

Pears are as fat as apples
They're crunchy like biscuits
Pears are as green as a leaf
They are as sweet as chocolate
They are as juicy as apples
They make me smile like the sun.

**Tawanda Kazembe (7)**
**Royston Primary School**

## Apple Poem

Apples are like oranges
Apples are as green as watermelons
They are red as a clown's nose
They are as yellow as the sun
Apples are healthy, like bananas
Apples are as crunchy as pears.

**Siam Adib (8)**
**Royston Primary School**

## Food Poem

I like curry with a little bit of spice
I like pies with a little bit of rice
I like pizza with tomato on top
I also like orange pop
I like carrot soup
With people in a group.

**Jake Wheeler (7)**
**Royston Primary School**

## Apple Poem

Apples are circular like a ball
They are as crunchy as a crisp
They are like an orange's shape
They are as sweet as corn
Apples are as nice as bananas.

**Chloe Wheeler (7)**
**Royston Primary School**

## My Food Poem

I found a shiny pear
It fell down from the windy air
Big grapes are the best
They help me to rest
I don't like sugary jelly
It isn't good for my small belly
I've heard of scrambled snake
It must give hungry people a bellyache
I like chicken curry
It puts me in a hurry
I like white milk
It looks like shiny silk.

**Tamara Bailey (8)**
**Royston Primary School**

## Pineapples

Pineapples are sticky like apples
They are sweet like mangoes
They are as spiky as roses
They are juicy like watermelons
Pineapples are as big as a head.

**Billy Best (7)**
**Royston Primary School**

## Orange Poem

An orange is round like a football
An orange is juicy like an apple
An orange is bright like the sun
An orange smells sweet
An orange is soft like a banana
An orange tastes juicy like a plum.

**Charlie Cox (7)**
**Royston Primary School**

## Apples

Apples are as juicy as oranges
Apples are hard like a wall
They can be red like tomatoes
They're round like the sun
They are sticky in the inside like bananas
Apples are as colourful as the Earth.

**Danilo Mrvaljevic (7)**
**Royston Primary School**

## A Victorian Child At Work

Darkness all around me
Dead rats falling along with piles of soot and dust
The echoes of my boss shouting unkind words up to me
The feeling of my boss poking me with a wooden stick.

Rats scuttling in the long, lush, green grass
The fear of the big black crows
The heavy wooden clapper weighing my arm down
The heavy rain pitter-pattering on me.

**Oliver Redmond (9)**
**St Andrew's Catholic Primary School, Streatham**

## A Victorian Child Worker

Life was very hard for a Victorian child
Working many hours, pushing coal from the mine
They got dirty and hot, but they never moaned or groaned
All for less than a pound, what a bad job!

**James Moran (9)**
**St Andrew's Catholic Primary School, Streatham**

## Chimney Sweep

Dirt and grime and green lime is what we see when we sweep
Birds and rats, soot and smoke
All of those things make us weep
Snow and rain
Dragging our feet
Going home is dreadful pain.

**Sean McGreevy (9)**
**St Andrew's Catholic Primary School, Streatham**

## The Old Victorian Mines

Some Victorian children worked in mines
And found it very hard
They worked their fingers to the bone
Until their feet moaned and groaned,
Without a word of praise.

They pulled carts of heavy black coal
And got beaten if they slept on the job,
They used all their strength
And never got anywhere.

I'm glad those days are over and done,
So we don't have to return to the times
Of the old Victorian mines.

**Alex Olivia Redman (9)**
**St Andrew's Catholic Primary School, Streatham**

## Victorian Children

Victorian children were stuck with gloom
In every working day of doom
Their boss would give them such a fright
They could not sleep throughout the night.

Then the Earl of Shaftesbury came
And made the children happy again
But when Queen Victoria passed away
There were still many children working
Long, long days.

**Daniel Alphonso (10)**
**St Andrew's Catholic Primary School, Streatham**

## A Scullery Maid's Day

5am - my day has begun,
I get my cold water jug,
My day ahead will not be fun,
I wish my attic had a rug.

I creep downstairs, as quiet as a mouse,
My friend Bessie by my side,
We light the fires in our master's house,
'The kitchen's so cold!' Bessie cried.

Our work is hard; we're the lowest of the low,
We are not allowed to talk,
We're scolded if we work too slow,
And we're told, 'Don't run, just walk!'

Midnight comes and I fall into bed,
At last I get some rest,
'Today was hard,' Bessie said,
But I know we did our best.

All too soon, the morning light,
Breaks through our windowpane,
We groan and sigh, as well we might,
As the whole thing starts again.

**Ellie Craven (10)**
**St Andrew's Catholic Primary School, Streatham**

## Victorian Children At Work

I stand out in the freezing cold,
Scaring the birds away,
With a wooden clapper I must hold,
I'm so lonely and sad each day.

I'm a skinny, weak stick insect,
Pulling coal through the mine,
When there's an explosion the mine gets wrecked,
Though a trapper's job is quite fine.

Fluffy, woolly clouds scatter,
The machinery bursts our ears
Some die and work should be safer,
Our hands are bloody through the years.

**Francesca Pereira (9)**
**St Andrew's Catholic Primary School, Streatham**

## The Elephant And The Hippo

*(Inspired by 'The Owl and the Pussycat' by Edward Lear)*

The elephant and the hippo went to Spain,
In an old Victorian car
They took a basket and some champagne
And an old Spanish guitar
Guitar, guitar
An old Spanish guitar.

They went to go and get a locket
In a long white car
They took a wallet in a big pocket,
They sang by the light of the stars
The stars, the stars,
They sang by the light of the stars.

**George Fitzgerald (9)**
**St Andrew's Catholic Primary School, Streatham**

## The Chimney Sweep

Nearly every day of the week
My job is a chimney sweep
The mess makes some people go, *'Eek!'*
It really means they want to weep.

I put all the soot in my sack
And clean up the mess on the floor
My face changes from white to black
And then I go out the door!

**Jake Hernandez (10)**
**St Andrew's Catholic Primary School, Streatham**

## Down In The Coal Mines

Down in the murky mines,
It's cramped and cold,
It's a scary place to work
When you're nine years old.

There's darkness all around us,
Like the blanket of night,
We pull the loaded trolleys,
We don't see a speck of light.

We pull the trolleys every day,
We use a metal chain,
It's hard and heavy around my waist,
It causes a lot of pain.

My stomach is very sick,
My hands are covered in dirt,
I haven't eaten a thing all day,
My back really does hurt.

I dream some day I will leave this mine,
Never to remember those sad days,
I have made some good friends down here,
But we will go our separate ways.

**Joseph Alford (10)**
**St Andrew's Catholic Primary School, Streatham**

## The Working Life Of A Victorian Child

I work in the coal mines,
With chains around my waist,
We pull coal in straight lines,
We always must make great haste.

The horribly heavy coal we heave,
Like mules we pull it all day
No sympathy do we receive,
How I wish I could just run away.

The ten-to-twelves are trusted,
To work with the pulley machine
The chains are rotten and rusted,
The miners are miserably mean.

My family are poor and need money,
Our clothes are all hand-me-downs
Outside I know it is sunny,
But my duty turns my smile to a frown.

The mines are as horrible as prison cells,
The very worst place I could be
Oh, please release me from this living hell,
I wish this wasn't happening to me.

**Prudence Gabriel (9)**
**St Andrew's Catholic Primary School, Streatham**

## A Bird-Scarer

My name is Elizabeth Jones
And I am ten,
I work in the fields freezing cold
To scare away birds and do as I am told.

I stand there all day watching away,
To make sure the birds do not stay,
I stand there all day, sometimes I pray,
That tomorrow will be a better day.

**Roisin Doherty (9)**
**St Andrew's Catholic Primary School, Streatham**

## The Life Of Victorian Children At Work!

We stand outside in the freezing field scaring birds away.
We have no food or shelter so we stand in the rain.
Some people come to check on us every single day.
If we do our job wrongly, we are smacked with a cane.
A cane.
If we do our job wrongly, we are smacked with a cane.

I really hate my job and we all have huge coats
Every day when I go to work I am very sad.
I get up early every morning so I can eat my oats.
My mum tells me I have to go to work and I can't see my dad.
My dad.
My mum tells me I have to go to work and I can't see my dad.

During my work I look up to the sky and pray for hope.
I wish I knew the time, I wish I had a clock.
Every day I have a feeling that I can't cope.
All day I walk with mud in each of my socks.
My socks.
All day I walk with mud in each of my socks.

**Sandra Ofili (9)**
**St Andrew's Catholic Primary School, Streatham**

## The Bird-Scarer

I am a bird-scarer and I scare birds away,
I get up at half-past five each day.
I get home at eight o'clock at night,
In the summer, it's just too bright.

In the wintertime,
In spite of cold and grime,
I scare the birds
By doing a mime.

**Uchenna Onyeji (10)**
**St Andrew's Catholic Primary School, Streatham**

## The Jumblies

They went to sea in a box they had,
Which could float and bob up and down,
They turned to go left but it went right instead,
But none of them gave a frown.

'Away we go!' shouted Pinkie Madoo.
'Ahoy!' yelled Gracie Vallor.
But the voyage was long and the sky was dark,
And they still did their jobs that they had to do!

At 9 o'clock they arrived safe and well,
Across from the River Atha Cliath,
So they spent the night in a pottery jar
And they had fish and chips for tea!

**Charlotte Hernandez (9)**
**St Andrew's Catholic Primary School, Streatham**

## The Servant

Muddy brown eyes and muddy brown hair, ugly clothes I get to wear,
I never see sunlight, I never see day;
I always work and never play (I wish I could every day),
I've got bruises on my leg, bruises on my face,
I am strong, stronger than two skates,
I'm just joking, I'm scared,
I am so scared, sometimes I even turn red.

**Adesua Okoeguale (9)**
**St Andrew's Catholic Primary School, Streatham**

## The Panda And Koala

*(Inspired by 'The Owl and the Pussycat' by Edward Lear)*

The panda and the koala went to Spain in a battered, old, yellow car
They took a game and some champagne and bought a brand new car
And bought a brand new car
New car
And bought a brand new car.

**Isabella Soares (9)**
**St Andrew's Catholic Primary School, Streatham**

## The Dog And Parrot

*(Inspired by 'The Owl and the Pussycat' by Edward Lear)*

The dog and parrot went out to eat,
On a rusty old telly
They took lots of money as the food was so yummy
And came back with a big old belly
A belly
And came back with a big old belly.

The dog and parrot started eating a carrot
On their way to Japan
They met a young man called smelly old Dan
Who hit himself with a pan
A pan
Who hit himself with a pan.

**Olivia Murphy (9)**
**St Andrew's Catholic Primary School, Streatham**

## Name

I wrote your name in the sky but the wind blew it away
I wrote your name in the sand but the water washed it away
I wrote your name in my heart and that's where it will stay.

**Dina Feseha (9)**
**St Andrew's Catholic Primary School, Streatham**

## The Dreadful Life Of A Bird-Scarer

I am a bird-scarer
I'm pale in the face
My lunch is lumpy slime
My life is a disgrace.

I own a wooden clapper,
I have a blocked nose
The field I work in is very plain
I can't even think about seeing a rose.

**Emilia Capitelli (10)**
**St Andrew's Catholic Primary School, Streatham**

## Working In A Coal Mine

On the 19th December
A contract was signed for me
To go and work in an old coal mine
Which was covered in yellow grime
And it was so dark you could hardly see
On a cold, wintry night
When it was as black as coal
Us children would sing
Would sing
Us children would sing.

Two days after I started working
My back started to have pain
And my hands were sore from opening doors
Also my bones ached from pulling the chains
I missed Mother and Father
And little Rosie too
I wished I could see them
See them
I wished I could see them.

**Megan Di Luzio (10)**
**St Andrew's Catholic Primary School, Streatham**

## Victorian Mine Trappers

Trappers worked in coal mines
They walked along the lines,
Deeper, deeper, deeper they walked into the coal mines.

Opening doors in front,
Closing them behind
Allowing nasty gases to escape the coal mines.

And when the day was over
They walked back up the lines
Higher, higher, higher, they walked out of the coal mines.

**Dejuan Markland (9)**
**St Andrew's Catholic Primary School, Streatham**

## Pulley Workers

My name is Peter Wallington
And I'm a pulley worker
And when I try to eat
I always get the choker.

Oh, why do I have to work?
I think you know why
But if I go to work
I feel like I'll die.

If I don't work fast enough
I'll get the cane
But, come on, it's so very tiring,
Do I have to handle the pain?

**Sammy Mehari (9)**
**St Andrew's Catholic Primary School, Streatham**

## A Young Schoolgirl

One poor little girl,
Went to school one morning
And was yawning,
Then felt appalling.

She was afraid of getting
The cane
She knew that
She would have pain,
She knew that she would have pain.

**Theresa Pillay (9)**
**St Andrew's Catholic Primary School, Streatham**

## A Trapper With No Attitude

Down in the deep, dark, cold mines,
There worked a trapper aged just nine,
He worked all day to earn a crust,
Cold and scared and covered in dust.
He opened and shut doors all day,
To keep the dangerous gases away.
Life was hard and his boss was cruel,
He couldn't even go to school.
He shivered with fright every day,
Making sure his whistling voice kept him awake,
Danger was around him everywhere
But this boy was so used to it he did not seem to care,
He did not see the point,
When he knew he would get hurt every day.
'Why waste my energy?' he would say,
'When I could be pleasing my master and get my pay.'

**Alice Beadle (10)**
**St Andrew's Catholic Primary School, Streatham**

## I'm A Young Bird-Scarer

I'm a young bird-scarer
And I'm eight years old
I'm paid five pence a day,
At least that's what I'm told.

I work in the fields, night and day
My type of play
Is chasing birds away all day.

I use a wooden clapper,
That's small but loud,
I don't really like it
Because of its sound.

I'm a bird-scarer
And I'm sorry to say
I'm sad to have to end this poem now
But I'll write to you another day.

**Sharlene Smith (9)**
**St Andrew's Catholic Primary School, Streatham**

## Monday's Child

Monday's child is as sweet as honey,
Tuesday's child is full of money
Wednesday's child is very grumpy,
Thursday's child hates porridge that is lumpy
Friday's child is full of joy
Saturday's child comes from the city of Troy
But the child that is born on the Sabbath day
Has her birthday in the month of May.

**Javiera Martinez (10)**
**St Andrew's Catholic Primary School, Streatham**

## A Victorian Child Worker

You wouldn't like to be a Victorian child
It's very, very tough
If you were one of us
You'd be doing hard stuff.

You'd be cleaning
Other people's dusty old shoes
Or sweeping chimneys
You never know whose.

You'd be working very late
Mending old socks
Helping poor Dad
Working at the docks.

Or helping your mum
Do some knitting
Or helping her cook
In the tiny cramped kitchen.

Or helping lift buckets
Up and down
And when you do that
I doubt it will be in a clean gown.

If you're a bird-scarer
You'd just be left alone
The first day you get there
You would want to go home.

**Amara Akande (9)**
**St Andrew's Catholic Primary School, Streatham**

## The Day The Zoo Escaped

The day the zoo escaped . . .
The monkey swung out cheekily
The spiders crawled out slickly
The tigers ran out viciously
The rabbits popped out poshly
The rats jumped out hopefully
The cheetahs zoomed out speedily
But the sloths dazily
Just ran around.

**Edward Obeng-Botah (10)**
**St Andrew's Catholic Primary School, Streatham**

## Domestic Servants

Domestic servants are we,
Only the rich people have glee.
We wish for things,
Like diamonds and rings
But little pay we get,
We get,
But little pay we get.

We sleep in small rooms,
And get out our brooms.
And we sweep the house at night,
At night,
And we sweep the house at night.

**Yasmin Campbell**
**St Andrew's Catholic Primary School, Streatham**

## Victorian Strife

Little Charlie was a Victorian working boy,
Who lived and worked on a farm,
On the purple moors;
He was not happy so he banged the doors,
His bed was dirty and he wore raggedy clothes.

As the sky became a painting of orange and red
The master said,
'Oh, you are a wretched boy.'
As he lay in bed in the dead of night,
The moon sailed by like a ghostly galleon,
He always dreamt that God saved him
From his life of strife and squalor.

**Amir Hyder (9)**
**St Andrew's Catholic Primary School, Streatham**

## Victorian Jobs

I stand in the field, lonely and scared,
Scaring the birds away from the corn,
My boss shouts at me from his house,
I have to wake up early in the morn.

I stand all day rubbing wool together,
While watching the massive machines go round
By the time I'm finished my hands are sore,
I wish I could sneak out without making a sound.

**Sinead Moran (9)**
**St Andrew's Catholic Primary School, Streatham**

## The Unicorn And The Serpent

*(Inspired by 'The Owl and the Pussycat' by Edward Lear)*

The unicorn and the serpent
Went to . . . Spain
In a cool convertible car.
They took a book and a candy cane
And said, 'We will go very far,
Very far.'
And said, 'We will go very far.'

When they got to Spain
They said, 'We're in pain.'
And went off to unpack
And after that they ate a snack
And said, 'We're going to hit the track,
The track.'
And said, 'We're going to hit the track.'

The serpent asked, 'Will you marry me?'
The unicorn thought about it.
She finally said, 'We shall see!
Maybe in a little bit,
A little bit.'

**Hannah Longley (9)**
**St Andrew's Catholic Primary School, Streatham**

## Working Days In A Mill

I see dust filling the air,
Children running for the wool,
The boss looks at us . . . he doesn't care!
'Turn on the machines!' he calls.
I can't hear. I'm deaf . . . I'm in the machine,
What will I have left?

I see children weeping . . . argh. I got through!
It is my best time . . . dinner time!
But really it's nothing new,
It is just the same thing, porridge or herbs.
At least I'm not working in the mines!
I have to hurry, I'm working a bit more,
It's actually the only way to get money, it's the law!

I'm working because I'm an apprentice,
I'm really tired, it's not my fault!
Well, I have to do it, it's on my list,
Wait a minute, I think the boss has just said halt!

**Danika Brereton (9)**
**St Andrew's Catholic Primary School, Streatham**

## Haunted By A Ghost!

It's peaceful and quiet until the night
I get such a fright
I hear her ghostly cry for freedom
But what can I do, I'm a child with no wisdom
She's a tearful ghost I tell you
When I see her she makes me go blue
When I ignore her, her voice gets deep
I get scared, but silence I wish to keep.

She surrounds me like a fence
And she goes really tense
Please, Mrs Ghost, leave me in peace
Please give me silence at least
Come on, Mrs Ghost, don't make me despair
I've got homework, this just isn't fair.

**Stephanie Etemewei (10)**
**St Joseph's Catholic Primary School, Rotherhithe**

## Happiness

Happiness smells like fresh-baked bread being cooked
in the finest oven.
It is the colour green like sweet lemon grass growing in fresh fields.
The feeling is like rubbing a newborn baby's skin.
It sounds like picking up your children from their first day
at primary school.
It reminds me of taking my first holy communion.
The feeling tastes like milk chocolate melting slowly in my mouth.
Happiness looks like a family photo that has been passed
through generations.

**Ekinadose Igbinoba (10)**
**St Joseph's Catholic Primary School, Rotherhithe**

## Laughter

Laughter smells like bubblegum-flavoured ice cream.
Laughter is the colour of bright yellow like the brightness of the sun
shining in the sky.
Laughter feels like England winning the World Cup.
It sounds like children playing in the park joyfully.
It reminds me of winning the lottery for my first time.
It tastes like a strawberry-flavoured lollipop.

**Jade Killick (10)**
**St Joseph's Catholic Primary School, Rotherhithe**

## Darkness

Darkness smells like a rotten egg lying in its cold bed.
Darkness is pitch-black like a night without stars.
Darkness feels like a werewolf creeping up behind you.
Darkness sounds like a little girl screaming in the woods.
Darkness reminds me of a scary nightmare.
Darkness tastes like dark chocolate.
Darkness looks like dark.

**Andres Torres (11)**
**St Joseph's Catholic Primary School, Rotherhithe**

## Laughter

Laughter is bright like a hot summer's day
It sounds like a little child who loves to play
It tastes like ice cream: vanilla and strawberry
It smells like rich and smooth hot honey
It looks like kids playing joyfully in the playground
It feels like being given fifteen million pounds
Laughter reminds me of the good old times.

**Michael Akinfisoye (10)**
**St Joseph's Catholic Primary School, Rotherhithe**

## Love

Love smells like a fresh red rose freshly picked from the finest garden
Love is lavender like a bride's bouquet
It feels like a silk robe which wraps around me
It sounds like an angel playing a harp in Heaven
It reminds me of my first kiss on the beach
It tastes like caramel melting slowly in my mouth
Love looks like my family.

**Reece Bayne (10)**
**St Joseph's Catholic Primary School, Rotherhithe**

## Sadness

Sadness is grey like a rainy October night
It tastes cold and bitter like a lemon ice lolly melting
It smells like smoke from the Twin Towers burning
It sounds like a cry for help when there is a bomb
It looks like a family watching at their friend's funeral
It reminds me of the tsunami that occurred in Thailand
It feels like when I remember the 7/7 bombing.

**Joseph Olaiya (10)**
**St Joseph's Catholic Primary School, Rotherhithe**

## Love

Love is as red as a gleaming colourful rose
It sounds like romance in the air on a special day called Valentine's Day
It tastes like mouth-watering chocolate that melts in your mouth
It smells like a room full of delightful spaghetti bolognese
It looks like God opening His hands to you
It feels like being hugged by your family
It reminds me of missing my family when I'm at school
It also reminds me of missing my great friends
And wonderful teachers when it's the weekend.

**Charlie Kiely (10)**
**St Joseph's Catholic Primary School, Rotherhithe**

## Fear

Fear is white like the horrific face of a menacing zombie.
It tastes like warm red blood trickling down my throat
It reminds me of being chased through an enchanted forest
by a ferocious dog
It feels like a gigantic shiver down my spine
It sounds like the haunting cackle of a frightening witch
It smells like the misty pitch-black air of an October night
It looks like the mouths of a thousand screaming people.

**Joel Christofi (10)**
**St Joseph's Catholic Primary School, Rotherhithe**

## Silence

Silence is white like the garments the two angels wore
When they told Mary Magdalene that Jesus was alive.
Silence looks like the black background you see when you're closing
your eyes in prayer.
Silence reminds me of what happened after Jesus died on The Cross.
Silence smells like the air you smell when the priest swings the incense.
Silence sounds like the stillness you feel
When you are receiving the Eucharist for the first time.
Silence is a calm sensation.

**Yolanda Kisenyi (11)**
**St Joseph's Catholic Primary School, Rotherhithe**

## Laughter

Laughter is as multicoloured as bright sunshine.
It sounds like a crazy bunch of hyenas laughing till the day they die
It tastes like succulent cake, just waiting for someone to eat it.
It smells like a rose, classic and fresh.
It looks like kids racing around the playground.
It feels like finding a million-pound cheque waiting for you to pick it up.
It reminds me of my friends when we all play our games.

**Bimpe Adeyemo (10)**
**St Joseph's Catholic Primary School, Rotherhithe**

## Silence

Silence is white as frozen snow.
It sounds like the wind going past your ears.
It tastes like a mouth-watering mouthful of hot chocolate,.
It smells like the sweet aroma of Mum's cooking.
It looks like a pillow.
It feels like I am just alone in a dark room.
It reminds me of when I pray to God.

**Adebowale Adenugba (10)**
**St Joseph's Catholic Primary School, Rotherhithe**

## My Dad

My dad is as big as a house
He is very tall
He can swim like a fish
He is as fast as a cheetah
He never lets you down if you need help
My dad is *great!*

**Eleni Christofi (7)**
**St Joseph's Catholic Primary School, Rotherhithe**

## My Sister Is Silly

My sister is silly
She says, 'OK.'
When my dad says, 'I'll give you a smack.'
When it's bedtime my sister does not want to go to bed
When it's morning, she wants to stay in bed
Just like an owl!

**Jack Roff (7)**
**St Joseph's Catholic Primary School, Rotherhithe**

## Sounds

The loudest sound in the world must be a blue wave crashing
in the sea
The weirdest sound in the world must be a zombie howling
madly with glee
The naughtiest sound in the world must be . . . me
The fluffiest sound in the world must be a squirrel chuckling
charmingly with me.

**Eren Ezel (8)**
**St Joseph's Catholic Primary School, Rotherhithe**

## Sound

The fastest sound in the world must be a cheetah running
madly towards me.
The meanest sound in the world must be a wrestler called
Big Show fighting me.
The coolest sound in the world must be Mr Platnum rapping
cheerfully a big bee.
The happiest sound in the world must be a gorgeous baby drinking
hot chocolate tea.

**Fisayo Adenugba (8)**
**St Joseph's Catholic Primary School, Rotherhithe**

## Sounds

The nicest sound in the world must be a red rose when it smiles
back at me.
The sweetest sound in the world must be a little butterfly
singing with me.
The largest sound in the world must be a flash of thunder lashing
right at me.
The sharpest sound in the world must be a knife nastily
trying to kill me.

**Conor Walsh (8)**
**St Joseph's Catholic Primary School, Rotherhithe**

## Sounds

The sweetest sound in the world must be a little baby squirrel taking
a nut slowly from me.
The softest sound in the world must be a little fuzzy animal
cuddling a tree.
The spookiest sound in the world must be a huge door squeaking
in the wind.
The best sound in the world must be a famous singer singing to me.
The naughtiest sound in the world must be a family of seagulls
taking my chips and tea!

**Tasha Lohan (8)**
**St Joseph's Catholic Primary School, Rotherhithe**

## Sounds

The loudest sound in the world must be a huge, hungry tiger racing
desperately for its tea.
The sweetest sound in the world must be a baby cub crying
for its mummy.
The smoothest sound in the world must be my friend singing
to God with me.
The spookiest sound in the world must be a ghost singing
horribly for me.
The quickest sound in the world must be a slug gasping
for its tasty tea.

**Sophie Metcalf (8)**
**St Joseph's Catholic Primary School, Rotherhithe**

## Sounds

The fastest sound in the world must be a speeding blue rocket
flying past me.
The meanest sound in the world must be a fat man spitefully
calling greedily.
The largest sound in the world must be a fierce lion roaring at me.
The spookiest sound in the world must be my hilarious dad singing
with glee.

**Mark Eastwood-Webb (8)**
**St Joseph's Catholic Primary School, Rotherhithe**

## The Witches' Spell

Mix together, stir and stew,
All ingredients to make a brew,
Crocodiles' lungs and oxen tongues,
Goat's liver and a cold-blooded river,
Scales of snakes and talons of eagles,
Creepy-crawlies and bat wings,
Mixed together these potent things,
Add tigers' claws and lions' teeth,
Red fish eyes and frogs' thighs,
Cut pigs' snouts while in their sties,
Stir and boil, the spell is cast,
The power is vast, it will last.

**Tessa Wade (10)**
**St Margaret's Lee CE School, Lewisham**

## All Hail

*(Based on Macbeth)*

*'All hail Macbeth,*
*Thane of Glamis,*
*All hail Macbeth,*
*Thane of Cawdor.*
*All hail Macbeth',*
Who shall be king of Scotland.
All hail Macbeth,
In all his honour and glory.

All hail Macbeth,
In all his disgrace and sin.
All hail Macbeth,
Who shall be driven to madness.
All hail Macbeth,
Who shall commit high treason.
All hail Macbeth,
Who shall become a murderer!

**Annalise Morley (11)**
**St Margaret's Lee CE School, Lewisham**

## Frogs And Snails

Frogs and snails and goats' tails,
Warthogs' limbs and crops that fail.
Lions' heads and chickens' guts,
Dogs' noses and pigs' butts.
Mice droppings and fishes' eyes
Cats' claws and birds baked in a pie
Where shall we meet?

In rain or in thunder,
In shock or in wonder,
In snow or in sun
In sadness or in fun,
In summer or in winter,
On our own or with a hinter.

**Chante Roach (10)**
**St Margaret's Lee CE School, Lewisham**

## I Love You

I love you, you love me
That's a happy family
With a great big hug
And a kiss from me to you
That means I love you.

**Melanie Da Silva Pinto (6)**
**Stockwell Primary School**

## A Half Of Fairy

A half of fairy is with one wing
A half of fairy is that it can sing
A half of fairy is that it can share love
A half of fairy is like a dove
A half of fairy is that it's a smash
A half of fairy is that you have to have the perfect match.

**Nekeshia McKenzie (8)**
**Stockwell Primary School**

## Black

My hat is black
My mat is black
My bats are black
My flute is black
My spot is black
My snot is black
My house is black
My mouse is black
Do you know what's
My favourite colour?

**Khaleda Islam (8)**
**Stockwell Primary School**

## Beat Of Time

Crash! Bash! Make a clash!
Smash! Crash! Bash and mash!
Click! Sick! Do a bit
Listen to the beat
But don't get sick
Listen to the music
Listen to the beat
Dance to the music
Get up on your feet
Listen to the beat of time
Come on and you will be fine.

Nash! Trash!
No need for a crash
It will only be a crash
Bash! Mash!
Bish! Bash!
Crash! Mash! Trash!
Don't make it all
A crash, bash, mash!
*Stop!*

**Shaquille Davis (9)**
**Stockwell Primary School**

## Roses

Roses are wonderful
They smell so powerful
When you smell the petals with your nose
You can feel the beat in your toes!
Roses are red, roses are blue
Roses are everything because
I dream of you!

**Natasha Ratnayake (10)**
**Stockwell Primary School**

## Hope

Hope brings strength
Strength brings love
Love brings songs
Love brings pain
Love stays forever
Love clearly needs a prayer.

**Danny Smith (10)**
**Stockwell Primary School**

## Butterflies

Butterflies are beautiful
Butterflies love flowers
Butterflies would fly around a garden for hours
Butterflies are colourful
With lots of different patterns
Butterflies come in different shapes
Colours and sizes
Because butterflies are beautiful
Butterflies are colourful
Butterflies are very pretty
Butterflies are wonderful.

**Nickandra Smith (10)**
**Stockwell Primary School**

## France

France is where I am from
France is where my family is from
And they still live there
With their big frizzy hair
France is where the kind wind goes past houses
France is about love and care.

**Jordan Abbah (9)**
**Stockwell Primary School**

## Summer Breeze

Summer breeze, so softly blowing,
In my garden pinks are growing,
If you go and send the showers,
You may come and smell my flowers.

**Jamal Bartley (9)**
**Stockwell Primary School**

## I Can See . . .

I have missed out on things today,
In fact, I miss out every day.
I can't see the flowers blooming in the sun,
I can't see when the day has begun.
I can't see traffic lights,
I can't see amazing sights.

But I can see a few things,
I can see people who are friendly and people that sing.
I can see people who are happy and kind,
I can see these things although I'm literally blind.
I don't see through my eyes you see,
I see through my head instead, that's me.

**Ellis Thomas (10)**
**Stockwell Primary School**

## Football

Football is my favourite sport,
I play for Fulham Academy,
On Thursdays and Saturdays too.
I also got into our school team,
Which made me want to jump and scream,
We won our first match, 2-1,
And I came on at half-time,
To play in defensive midfield
And played well.
Our league is 10 matches
And ends in February.
If we win it,
We'll get a humungous trophy to keep at school
And gold medals to keep at our house!
*Yah!*

**Tesfa Atere (9)**
**Stockwell Primary School**

## The Best Gift Ever

It was my birthday
I went downstairs to the living room
I saw lots of gifts near the computer
I ran to the corner to rip open my gifts
First I opened this bright red one with blue ribbons
And it was a talking dolly
I ran round the house and said, 'I love this toy
I always wanted this, it's the best gift ever.'

**Shannon Jackson (10)**
**Stockwell Primary School**

## When A Fairy Is Born

When a fairy is born, she has one wing
When a fairy is born, she must have a twin
So they can make twin magic
If you have never seen a fairy
It's because she's waiting for the right time
But most people don't believe
And listen to rhythm and rhyme.

A fairy has trust in you
And if you believe hard enough
Your wishes come true
But don't give up
Because some wishes are due
But when a twin fairy is born
She looks like you.

**Jaydene Reece-Gardner (8)**
**Stockwell Primary School**

## Chocolate

Chocolate stops me feeling lonely
It talks to me like my best friend
It makes me feel happy
It is my only sister
I just love chocolate
Like it's my family.

**Alice Postans (10)**
**Stockwell Primary School**

## Laughter

Laughter is pink because it's bright and beautiful
Laughter sounds like people jumping around laughing and chatting
Laughter tastes like lemon, apple and oranges
The lemon, apple and oranges smell like laughter
It looks like a chorus singing at the funfair
It feels really happy, laughing around
It reminds me of me and my cousin swimming.

**Kelly Tran (9)**
**Stockwell Primary School**

## Drink

If your horrid little brother
Offers you a drink
Just think
Before you drink
It could be ink.

**Tonicha Hilder (9)**
**Stockwell Primary School**

## What Is Yellow?

Yellow is a sunny day,
When all troubles melt away.
Yellow makes me feel so happy,
Yellow is so fun,
Yellow is the colour of the sun.
Yellow is very hot in June,
I hope I get to see it soon.
Yellow is my fellow,
Yellow is warm sunshine,
It makes me feel fine.
Yellow is the colour of hay,
Which I would like to sleep in one day.

**Neev Trehan (8)**
**Stockwell Primary School**

## The Clock

Different shapes and sizes
Always on the go
It always moves when it chooses
Never cracks a smile
Without moving a mile
Never eats or speaks
Or gives you a treat
Sees everything you do
Without having a clue
On and on, tick-tock
The alarm just wakes up your whole block.

**Hassan Mugga (10)**
**Stockwell Primary School**

## The World Is Talking To Me

When I was walking the trees were talking
The doves were working in the tree
It was strange I did not know what was happening to me
Snowflakes were bubbling up
The cows were mooing at me
The wind was saying hello to me
Everything was driving me crazy.
Swimming through the sea, waves pushing at me
Is this all a dream?
What does it mean?

**Kevaun McKenzie (10)**
**Stockwell Primary School**

## Laughter

Pink is the colour of laughter which stands for happiness
Laughter sounds like clowns coming out of the air and telling
you to laugh
Laughter tastes sweet so you can taste like strawberry sweets
and laugh at people
Laughter smells like clowns and you start to laugh
Laughter looks like clowns are doing funny things to make you laugh
Laughter feels like clowns are sitting next to you
And talking to you about funny things to make you laugh
Laughter reminds you of when someone does something
They have to make you really laugh.

**Diana Sam (9)**
**Stockwell Primary School**

## Love

Love is the greatest thing
Some think it's big
I care about love
It is a dove
Love is good
Love is great
Love knows what it's doing
Love is the Earth
Love is a new bright birth
Love is all I have
And I am so glad!

**Sashalee Biggs (8)**
**Stockwell Primary School**

## Pain

Pain is the colour of red for blood
And looks like a doll because it is dead
Pain sounds like *bang! Bang! Bang!*
Pain is like you're hurt in the bed
The smell of pain is like chilli sauce
And pain reminds me of the film 'Matrix Path of Neo'
Pain feels like you are on fire
And pain all happens to Theo.

**Arifur Rahman (8)**
**Stockwell Primary School**